WHERE I LIVE

In a City

Honor Head

WAYLAND

Explore the world with **Popcorn** - your complete first non-fiction library.

Look out for more titles in the Popcorn range. All books have the same format of simple text and striking images. Text is carefully matched to the pictures to help readers to identify and understand key vocabulary.
www.waylandbooks.co.uk/popcorn

First published in 2010 by Wayland
Copyright © Wayland 2010

Wayland
Hachette Children's Books
338 Euston Road
London NW1 3BH

Wayland Australia
Level 17/207 Kent Street
Sydney NSW 2000

Produced for Wayland by
White-Thomson Publishing Ltd
www.wtpub.co.uk
+44 (0)843 208 7460

Editor: Jean Coppendale
Designer: Clare Nicholas
Commissioned photography: Chris Fairclough
Picture Researcher: Amy Sparks
Series consultant: Kate Ruttle
Design concept: Paul Cherrill

With thanks to Joel and his friend Jamie, and Joel's family,
for their help with this book.

British Library Cataloging in Publication Data
Head, Honor.
   In a city. -- (Popcorn. Where I live)
   1. City and town life--Great Britain--Pictorial works--Juvenile literature.
   I. Title II. Series
   941'.009732-dc22

ISBN: 978 0 7502 6318 4

Wayland is a division of Hachette Children's Books,
an Hachette UK company.
www.hachette.co.uk

Printed and bound in China

Photographs:
Dreamstime: Stephen Bures 13/22; Shutterstock:
Pres Panayotov 5, Stephen Finn 20

Contents

The city

My name is Joel. I live in a city
called London. The building where
I live used to be a big house.
It has been changed to three flats.

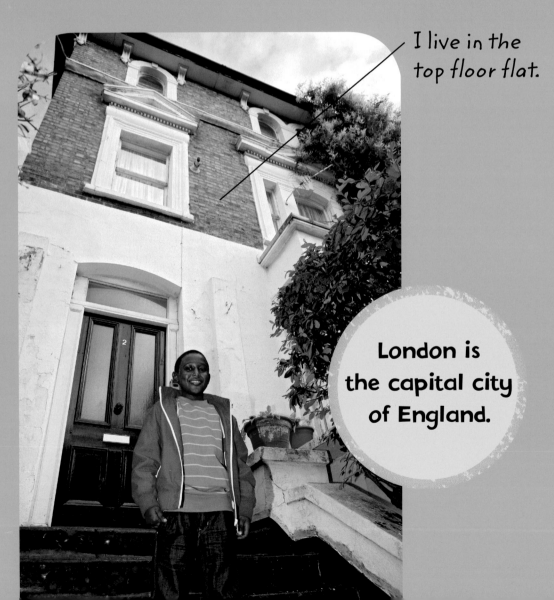

I live in the
top floor flat.

London is
the capital city
of England.

The city is a big place where
lots of people live and work.
It can be very busy and noisy.

block of flats

There are lots of
blocks of flats in
the city because
so many people
need somewhere
to live.

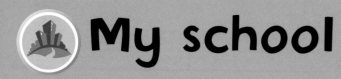

My school

My school is near to where
I live. It has seven classrooms,
a playground and a garden.

My friend Jamie and I
go to the same school.

Sometimes we go on a school outing. We go to a museum or an art gallery. My favourite is the Science Museum.

What do you think you can see in the Science Museum?

After school

Sometimes after school Dad takes me and Jamie to the park. Here there is a marked area where we can play football.

Football is fun and great exercise after school.

There is also a playground at the park. I like the climbing frame best.

What do you like to do at the playground?

The high street

My house is near the high street. This is a main road that has lots of shops and other buildings such as banks.

People who don't live nearby can take a bus to the high street.

bus stop

Mum buys her fruit and vegetables from the greengrocer in the high street. I help her to choose some fruit for my lunchbox.

Which fruit can you see in this shop?

Getting around

Many buses stop in the high street.
Some are for short journeys only.
Others take you all over the city.

You have to buy
a ticket from the
machine before
you get on the bus.

There is also an underground station nearby where we can catch a tube train. The tube is usually quicker than a bus.

In the mornings and evenings the underground is very busy.

The time when people are going to work and coming home is called the rush hour.

13

Commuting

Many people work in the city centre. They travel by overground train to the city centre. From here they walk, or catch a bus, tube or taxi to where they work.

Charing Cross station has overground and tube trains.

Some commuters drive into the city by car.

There are big modern office
blocks in the city centre.
Some office blocks are so big that
hundreds of people work there.

Modern office blocks
have big windows to
let in lots of light.

Tourists

There are always lots of tourists and visitors in the city centre. Some are on holiday and some come because of their work.

Tourists like to visit places such as Trafalgar Square.

Tourists come from overseas and other parts of Britain.

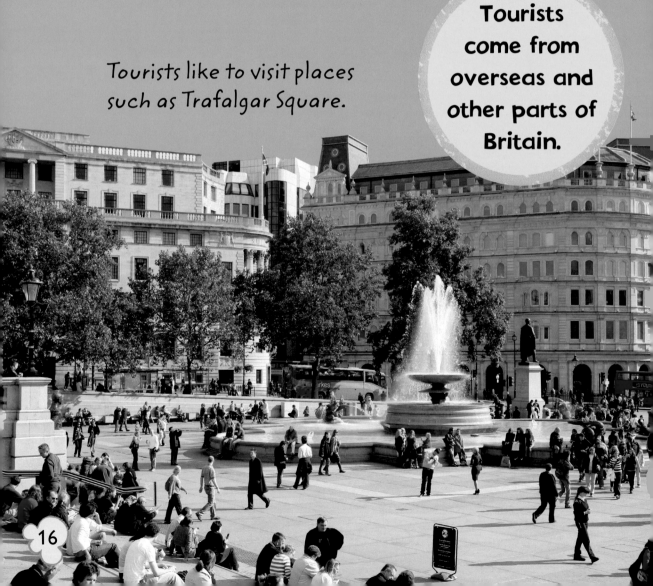

There is a special tourist bus that takes people sightseeing. They go to places of interest in the city.

The tourist bus has an open top so that people can see more of the city.

The River Thames

One of the places I like to visit is the River Thames. This is a river that runs right through the middle of the city.

There are boat trips on the River Thames.

There are lots of restaurants, cafes and shops along the river. Sometimes there are people playing music. These are called buskers.

No cars are allowed along the river side so it is safe to walk.

Shopping

At the weekend we sometimes go to the shopping centre. We drive there in the car and park in the multi-storey car park.

The multi-storey car park has lots of different floors for the cars to park on.

At the shopping centre all the shops are under a big roof. This means we can enjoy shopping even if the weather is bad.

There are lots of different shops, restaurants and cafes at the shopping centre.

A day in the city

Match the pictures to the sentences to remember some things you can do in the city.

1. Go shopping in the high street.
2. Visit a museum.
3. Go on the underground train.
4. Take a boat trip on the River Thames.
5. Have a sightseeing tour on a special bus.

Glossary

banks buildings where people go to save their money or borrow money

buskers people who play music on the street and hope that people passing by will give them some money

city a large place where lots of people live and work

greengrocer a shop that sells fresh fruit and vegetables

multi-storey a place that has many floors

places of interest usually old historical buildings, museums, art galleries and statues that people visiting a city want to see

sightseeing when tourists visit places of interest

tourists people who travel to a place where they don't live

Index

Where I Live

Contents of titles in the series:

WAYLAND